Kids' Gardening

Kids'
Gardening

Susie Johns

p

This is a Parragon Publishing Book

Parragon Publishing
Queen Street House
4 Queen Street
Bath BA1 1HE, UK

Copyright © Parragon 2001

Designed, produced and packaged by
Stonecastle Graphics Ltd

Text by Susie Johns
Edited by Gillian Haslam
Design by Sue Pressley and Paul Turner
Projects by Susie Johns
Photography by Roddy Paine
Art Direction by Sue Pressley and Paul Turner
Illustrations by Paul B. Davies

ISBN 0-75258-872-9

Printed in China

Contents

Introduction

Gardening is one of the best and most exciting ways to be in touch with nature. Follow the projects in this book and not only will you have lots of fun but you will learn about germination, transpiration, and many of the other miracles of horticulture.

Find out how to grow plants from seed or cuttings, how to create a miniature garden in a box and how to cultivate your very own crops of beans, strawberries, tomatoes, and herbs.

If you are lucky enough to have a garden, perhaps there is a sunny patch you will be allowed to call your own. Even if the garden is small and there is no ground to spare, you can grow all kinds of plants in pots, tubs, and baskets. And even if you live in an apartment, a corner of a balcony or a sunny windowsill will offer you the chance to experiment with container-grown plants. Success in growing your very own pot of parsley or creating a mini cactus garden is enough to be able to call yourself a gardener!

What does it cost?

Gardening can cost next to nothing, as most of the projects in this book will show. A packet of seeds, at a pocket-money price, will yield an abundance of flowers or vegetables. A small tomato plant bought at a market or school fair will grow, if properly cared for, into a tall plant heavy with ripe fruits. Cuttings can be taken from plants already in the garden, to make new plants from old. And at the end of the summer, seed can be gathered from fading plants for next year's planting.

Although a garden may include lots of edible plants, please remember that not all plants can be eaten and some may even be poisonous. Always double-check with a grown-up before eating anything you pick from the garden – even if you have grown it yourself!

Gardening Basics

Gardening tools

For the small-scale projects in this book, a trowel and rake are useful but you could just as easily manage with an old spoon and fork. Long ago, people cultivated whole fields with only makeshift tools such as sticks, seashells, stones, and bones.

A watering can is useful but you can improvise. An old plastic bottle will do just as well. For a fine sprinkling of water, stretch cling film over the top and pierce a few holes in it with a pin.

A notebook is handy for writing down information, sticking in seed packets, and making drawings of your plants at various stages in their development.

Use a tape measure or ruler to measure growth or to help space out seeds or plants in the ground.

Sticks help to support tall or climbing plants such as beans, sweet peas, tomatoes, and sunflowers. Buy some pea sticks or bamboo canes from the garden center, or use sticks trimmed from trees or bushes, as long as you have permission. Gently tie the plants to the sticks with garden string or wire ties.

A sheet of clear plastic can also be used to make a temporary greenhouse. Simply lay it on top of a couple of bricks and place the plant pots underneath.

Soil

For growing seeds and planting in containers, special compost mixtures, available from garden centers, will give you the best results. Sand and gravel are also useful, and

you will need some pebbles or broken pieces of clay pots to assist drainage in containers.

Plastic cups and soft drink bottles are useful as protective shields for young plants or as mini propagators (cut the bottoms off the bottles and place them over the plants – the sunlight can still reach them and they will be kept extra warm).

It your pocket money will not stretch to buying lots of different bags of compost, one bag of general purpose compost should be suitable for most of the projects in this book.

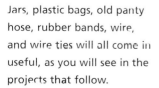

Jars, plastic bags, old panty hose, rubber bands, wire, and wire ties will all come in useful, as you will see in the projects that follow.

Containers

You can be very creative with containers for plants. Almost anything – a cup, a colander, a basket, or a wooden crate – can be used.

If the container has no holes in the base, and you are unable to make any, make sure you put a generous layer of pebbles or gravel in first. A lightweight alternative is broken pieces of polystyrene packaging. This layer will allow water to drain to the bottom of the container so the soil does not remain too wet.

If your container does have drainage holes, place a few pebbles or pieces of broken clay pot over the holes so that water – but not soil – can drain out.

Plant labels

If you are growing a number of plants, don't rely on your memory to remember what they are – make your own labels. Save wooden popsicle sticks and write plant names on them with permanent marker pens. Collect smooth, flat stones and paint names using acrylics. For indoor plants, make paper flags with cocktail sticks or kebab skewers.

Bug patrol

If you are growing edible plants in the garden, it is advisable not to use chemical herbicides, fungicides and pesticides, or slug pellets.

Pick pesky bugs, such as slugs and snails, off your plants by hand, or blast away greenfly or blackfly by squirting them with a jet of water. But leave caterpillars, if you can, to give them a chance to grow into butterflies.

To prevent slimy slugs from attacking your young plants, you could try this trick. Cut out the base from a plastic cup, slip the cup over the plant and push the rim into the ground so it forms a mini fortress. Leave in place for a few weeks while the plant grows stronger.

Another effective slug trap is to place halved grapefruits or oranges between the plants (scoop out the flesh and eat it first). The slugs will crawl in, so you can remove them easily.

Food and drink

Don't let your plants go through a long, hot summer's day without water – give them a drink! Do this first thing in the morning or in the evening. It is best to water the ground round the base of the plant, rather than the stems or the leaves.

Most plants also benefit from feeding – particularly those grown in containers, where nutrients (the goodness in the soil) are limited. For food, use garden compost, prepared manure, or maybe a seaweed fertilizer. Your local garden center will be able to give you advice. Always take care when using fertilizer and keep it in a safe place.

Weeding

If you have your own patch of garden, you may find plants growing there that you haven't cultivated. Ask a grown-up to help you identify which plants are weeds, then pull them up and dispose of them on a compost heap or in the garbage. If left to grow, they could take over and prevent your plants from growing properly.

Keep a diary

Write down what you planted and the date. Record the heights of sunflowers as they grow. Weigh a crop of tomatoes. Keep a note of what has grown best, so you can repeat your success next year.

Safety Tips

• Never eat berries, seeds, or 'mushrooms' – they could be poisonous.

• Always wash your hands after gardening.

• Ponds must be totally inaccessible to small children. They can drown if they fall into the water.

• Chemical pesticides and fertilizers are harmful. Store them safely and dispose of empty containers with care. Never use them without asking a grown-up first.

• Ask a grown-up to help when handling wire (you could cut yourself), lifting heavy objects (you could drop them), or pulling up weeds (they may be precious plants).

Outdoor Projects

Time of Year – spring

Springtime Window Box

Brighten up a windowsill with a boxful of pretty plants. With a bit of careful planning, you can have year-round color.

Choose a few long-lasting plants for your window box, such as ivy, heathers, and small conifers. Then add colorful seasonal flowers in the gaps. Primulas are a perfect choice for early spring.

You will need
- suitable container, with drainage holes
- pebbles or broken clay pots • gravel
- potting compost • choose from ivy plants, dwarf conifers, heathers, primulas, and violas

1
Put pebbles or pieces of broken clay pot in the base of your window box, then a layer of gravel. Half-fill the box with compost.

2
Carefully remove plants from their pots and, if the roots look a bit squashed, gently tease them out with your fingers.

3
Place all your plants in the window box, leaving a bit of space around each one to allow for growth.

Are you satisfied with the arrangement? It is best if tall plants (conifers) are put at the back and trailing ones (ivy) at the front. Now fill the gaps around each plant with more compost. Press the compost down with your fingers so your plants are firm and secure.

4

SPRING INTO SPRING

In fall or winter, plant pansies – and why not bury some bulbs in the soil as well? Choose crocuses, hyacinths, or narcissi. Put your pansies in position, then place the bulbs, pointed ends upward, in between. Add compost to within $3/4$in (2cm) of the rim of the box. The bulbs should be covered completely. The pansies will provide color all winter and then, in spring, the bulbs will flower.

• Water your plants before you remove them from their pots. After planting, water the window box immediately, then water every day.

• Plants like a clean home. If your window box or other container has been used before, wash it thoroughly with warm, soapy water before you plant it up.

• A window box is heavy once it has been filled with compost – perhaps too heavy to lift. Either place your box in position on the windowsill before planting or ask a grown-up to help you to move it and ensure it will not fall off the windowsill.

• In summer, instead of primulas you could plant geraniums, petunias, or *Impatiens*. Maybe you could use some plants you have grown from seeds or cuttings?

Time of Year – spring

Hanging Basket

A metal colander is the perfect choice for a hanging basket, with ready-made drainage holes. Plant it with pansies in the colors of your choice, then water it every day and your efforts will be rewarded with a cascade of color.

You will need
- suitable container (see box)
- liner (see box)
- bucket or bowl
- potting compost
- 5 or 6 pansy plants
- chain or wire, for hanging

1 Stand the colander on a bucket or bowl if necessary, so it does not rock about. Line the colander if you wish (see box), then half-fill with compost.

2 Remove the pansy plants carefully from their pots and arrange them on the compost, spacing them out evenly.

3 Fill the gaps with compost and firm it down. Water gently.

• Petunias also come in a wonderful range of colors. You can even get striped ones! Choose plants of all one color, or a multicolored assortment. You could also try *Impatiens*, verbena, or geraniums, or a combination.

• Even though your basket may not look very impressive when you first plant it, the plants will soon grow strong and bushy, filling out all the gaps and producing a stunning display of colorful flowers that should last all summer long if you take care of them.

AN INTERESTING CONTAINER

Instead of an old colander, you may have other suitable containers around the house, such as an old wicker basket, a wire vegetable basket, an old bird cage, or a bucket that a grown-up can punch holes in. Of course, you can buy hanging baskets from a garden center – but it is much more fun to make use of something you have found!

CHOOSING A LINER

Hanging baskets tend to dry out quickly so you will have to look after your plants, watering them daily. A liner will help to retain moisture. Line the container with a piece of plastic cut from a bin liner, with holes pierced in it to let some of the water out so the compost does not become waterlogged. Or buy some moss, a compressed paper liner, or special fibrous matting.

4

Add lengths of chain or wire for hanging. Hang your basket in a sunny spot but not too high up or you will not be able to reach it with your watering can!

Taking Cuttings

This is a clever way to grow plants for free. Ask friends and family to donate cuttings from their own plants. Start with geraniums, which are easy to cultivate using this method.

You will need
- geranium (pelargonium)
- scissors
- potting compost
- sand
- glass jar with lid

1

Cut a small stem from a geranium. Cut it below a leaf joint – that is, where leaves branch out from the stem.

2

Mix some potting compost with a little sand in a glass jar. Push the cutting into the soil, firming down all around it.

EASY TO GROW

Try growing other plants from cuttings. *Impatiens* can be grown in exactly the same way as geraniums.

Or cut pieces of mint or small stems of ivy and place them in a jar of water.

As soon as roots appear, you can plant the cutting in a pot of compost.

3

Add a few drops of water and screw on the lid. Stand the jar on a sunny windowsill and within a few weeks you should see fine roots pushing through the soil.

Animal Ivy

Time of Year – spring

Make an ornamental
animal in a pot. By growing
ivy over a wire framework,
you can be really creative.

You will need
• garden wire • wire cutters
• large flower pot or similar
container • ivy plants

1

Bend a length of wire into a simple
animal shape – a duck, a cat, or perhaps
a fish, for example. Carefully twist the
ends of the wire together at the
bottom, so as to make a stake that can
be pushed into the soil. You may need
to ask a grown-up to help you with this
stage of the project as the ends of the
wire can be very sharp.

2

Fill a pot with compost (remembering
to include some drainage material in
the bottom of the pot). Stick the wire
frame into the soil.

PLANTS FOR FREE

Instead of buying plants, cut stems from ivy already growing in your garden (or ask a friend or neighbor for cuttings). Place stems in water until roots start to appear. This can take as little as a few days in warm weather. Then plant your ivy stems, as in step 3.

3

Dig holes in the soil around the wire frame and plant ivies. (See page 17 for planting tips.) Carefully wind the ivy stems around the wire and in and out of the framework.

As the ivy grows it will cover the frame and create a leafy animal. From time to time, tuck stray stems into the framework, or trim off leaves or stems that cannot be trained.

Time of Year – anytime

Desert Garden

By combining cacti and succulents in a shallow
container, you can create a little oasis in a bowl.

Choose a shallow container (see the miniature
garden on page 26), such as a terracotta bowl.
It is important to choose plants that enjoy similar
growing conditions. Look for fleshy-leaved succulents
that store water in their roots, stems, and leaves,
combining them with cacti which
like dry, sunny conditions and
will survive quite well even
if you neglect them. To add
a touch of color, you can
cover exposed areas of soil
with aquarium gravel.

You will need
- shallow container
- small pebbles or gravel
- compost (buy a special mixture suitable for succulents and cacti)
- plants
- gardening gloves
- colored gravel

1

Put a layer of gravel
in the bottom of the
container, then half-
fill it with compost.

2

Carefully remove the plants from their pots and position on the surface of the soil. Move them around until you are happy with the arrangement, then fill the spaces between the plants with compost.

3

When all the plants are planted, scatter the coloured gravel over the surface of the soil.

4

Place the container in a sunny position such as a windowsill.
Water it sparingly, sprinkling water around the edges so the centre does not become waterlogged.

For a great decorative effect, fill a large glass container with layers of sand, gravel and compost to create a striped design. In a smaller container, plant just one or two cacti or succulents.

Time of Year – late spring or summer

Miniature Landscape

Small plants arranged in a shallow container can look like a garden that has been magically reduced in size, especially if you add a pond and some little animals.

You will need
- large, shallow container (*see box*)
- gravel
- potting compost
- small foil dish or aluminum can
- trowel or old spoon
- small plants (*see box*)
- pebbles and seashells
- plastic animals

1 Start by placing a layer of gravel in the bottom of the container, to help drainage, then fill the container to within $3/4$in (2cm) of the rim with potting compost. Sink a dish or can into the compost, to make a pond.

2 Using your trowel or spoon, dig small holes and put in your plants. A dwarf conifer will look like a small tree. If you have a trailing plant, such as thyme, place it near the edge so it will tumble over the rim.

3

Add a few pebbles and seashells, especially around the edge of the pond. Fill in gaps between plants with a little gravel. Add plastic animals or other toys for decoration.

BE CREATIVE WITH CONTAINERS

You could use a shallow clay trough, a plastic washing-up bowl or cat litter tray, a wooden fruit crate, or a basket lined with a plastic bag.

Suggested plants

Rock cress (aubrietia), gold dust (alyssum), thyme, candytuft, dwarf pinks, and dwarf conifers are all suitable and easy to care for. Look in the alpine section at your local garden center and ask staff there to recommend tiny, pocket-money plants.

SPRING GARDEN

For a miniature spring garden, plant small bulbs such as dwarf iris, crocus, narcissi, and snowdrops in late fall, covering them with compost and a layer of moss. Stick a few bare twigs and stones into the moss, then wait until spring.

Garden Hideaway

If you have ever wanted your very own
garden hideaway, then this could be just what you have
been looking for. It's really easy to make – all you need is
some bamboo canes, some string, and some pole bean seeds
– and not only will it look great, you will be able to harvest
a crop of tasty pods and eat them for dinner!

1

On a spare area of
garden soil, about 1.5m
by 5ft x 5ft (1.5m) mark
out the square shape of
your hideaway with four
upright bamboo canes.

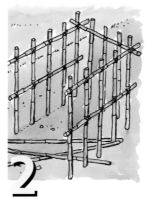

2

Place equally spaced
upright canes around
three of the sides, leaving
one side open. Tie more
canes across the sides and
the top to make the roof.

3

Once the danger of frost
has passed, sow seeds 2in
(5cm) deep, at the base of
each cane. Water in well
to assist germination and
watch the plants grow!

Time of Year – early summer

As the plants grow, train them to wind their way up the canes and across the top of your hideaway to create a really secluded den.

• Remember to keep the plants well watered, especially on hot, dry summer days.

• You will enjoy a super display of beautiful flowers followed by the growth of many pole bean pods.

• Pick the beans regularly to ensure the plant continues to produce more pods.

• You don't have to follow our design exactly. You could make the frame into a wigwam or grow climbing annual flowers instead of pole beans.

FAST FACTS

Pole beans come from the tropical parts of America, so it's no surprise that they like their roots to be in warm soil and will grow well in a nice sunny position. They grow very fast – you could have a plate of beans in just seven weeks!

Save some seeds and dry them for next year.

Super Sunflowers

These bright, beautiful flowers grow like magic. In fact, when a sunflower is full-grown, it may well be taller than you!

You can plant seeds directly in the garden soil, in the exact position you want your sunflowers to grow. Choose a sunny spot!

Be sure to water your seeds every day.

As your sunflowers grow, you may need to give them some support. Push a tall cane into the ground next to the sunflower and use garden string to tie the stem loosely to the cane.

Time of Year - spring

• Why not have a competition with a friend or brother or sister to see who can grow the tallest sunflower? Plant the seeds at the same time, so you all get off to a fair start, then record the plants' growth in your garden notebook.

• The center of the large flower head is made up of masses of seeds. Even after the petals have withered, leave the flower and its seeds to dry out in the sunshine. Save some to plant next year and leave the rest for the birds to eat.

• Why not plant seeds in yogurt pots – one seed to each pot (see pages 42–43). Water them and look after them carefully until they grow into small plants, then transfer them to the garden. You could give them away as presents or sell them at the school fair.

• If you do not have a garden, you can still grow a sunflower. Tall varieties need a large pot and plenty of space to grow. Or choose a smaller type, such as *Helianthus debilis*, which will not need as much space.

Time of Year – late spring

Grow Your Own Tomatoes

Plant tomatoes in late spring for a September crop. Watch your plants grow all summer long, see the fruits develop, ripen, and magically change color from green to red.

You will need
- growing bag
- 4 or 5 tomato plants
- scissors
- trowel or spoon

1 Put the growing bag in a flat, sunny place in the garden or on a sunny balcony. Cut crosses in the top layer of plastic, one for each plant.

2 Peel back the plastic in the places where you have cut it and dig planting holes in the compost.

3 Gently remove the plants from their pots. Place one in each hole and firm down the soil. Water well.

• Choose a variety of tomato that is easy to grow: Moneymaker or Alicante are good ones. Instead of buying plants, you can grow your own from seed. See page 43 for tips on germination.

Nip out any side shoots which start to grow and pinch out the growing tip after the plant has formed five trusses of fruit. This will encourage more fruits to develop and prevent the plant from becoming tall and straggly.

GROWING BAG

A growing bag is a special long, flat plastic sack filled with compost. Rather than tipping the compost into pots, you grow the plants in the sack. However, if you do not have a growing bag, plant tomatoes in large flower pots or similar containers, one or two to each container. As soon as your plants begin to produce little shoots, you will need to feed them with a liquid tomato feed diluted in water (follow the instructions on the bottle and ask a grown-up to help).

• As your tomato plants grow, the little shoots (called trusses) will develop flowers. Then watch as each flower becomes a little tomato. Remember to water the plants regularly.

Time of Year – late spring

Strawberry Tower

Garden centers sell special tall pots with holes down the sides as well as at the top specially for growing strawberries. They can be expensive, so here is a way of creating your own strawberry tower using ordinary flowerpots.

You will need
- 3 flowerpots, different sizes
- pebbles or broken clay pots
- potting compost
- trowel or spoon
- strawberry plants

SMALL IS BEAUTIFUL

When buying plants, choose varieties that are small and suitable for growing in containers. They will need a rich potting compost, regular feeding, and lots of sunshine. Water when the compost starts to dry out but do not overwater as this will encourage mildew.

1

After placing some drainage pebbles or broken pots in the bottoms, fill the flowerpots with compost to within ³/4in (2cm) of the rims. Place the pots on top of one another, the largest at the bottom, pushing the others down firmly into the compost so they do not topple over.

• To prevent birds from stealing the strawberries, protect your plants with a shield of fine mesh netting. An old net drape will do the trick.

• Strawberries can also be grown in a window box or a hanging basket.

2

Dig planting holes in the soil, big enough to accommodate the roots of the strawberry plants. Tip each one out of its pot and gently tease out the roots. Position the plants at a slight angle, pointing out from the pots, so they will trail down the sides. Water the plants well.

Time of Year – spring/summer

Dress a Scarecrow

This is a traditional way of trying to stop birds stealing newly planted seeds. Fun to make from old clothes, put one in your vegetable patch and see if it frightens the birds away!

You will need
- 2 broom handles or heavy sticks
- string • old clothes
- newspapers
- permanent marker pen
- straw or hay

1 Place one broom handle across the other, to form a cross. Tie them firmly together with string.

2 To make the head, stuff a cloth bag or an old T-shirt with newspaper, push the top of the broom handle inside and tie around the neck with string. Draw a face on the head with the pen.

3 Stuff the sleeves of a shirt or jacket with newspapers. Put it on your scarecrow and fasten any buttons. Stuff straw into the ends of the sleeves.

• Another way to scare birds from your seed patch is to suspend a length of string across the garden and hang objects from it such as strips of plastic and foil, bottle tops, and bells. As they move in the breeze, they will frighten the birds.

• Of course, although you don't want birds to eat your seeds before they have had a chance to grow, you do want to encourage birds to visit your garden – so turn the page to discover some ways to do this.

MINI SCARECROW

Just for fun, you could make a mini scarecrow for a window box or other container.

Bind together two sticks to form a cross, and make a head from a small square of fabric stuffed with paper or straw. Place some straw along the arms and bind it in place with string. You could even add a doll-sized jacket and hat!

4

Put a hat on the scarecrow and stuff some straw under the brim as hair.

Bird Feeder

To attract birds to your garden, you need to provide them with food, water, and shelter. Here is a recipe for a special cake that birds will love to eat. You may need to ask a grown-up to help with melting the lard.

You will need
- 8oz (225g) lard
- 16oz (450g) mixed foods, such as stale bread or cake, bacon rinds, hard pieces of cheese, dried fruits, unsalted nuts, or coconut

1 Melt the lard in a saucepan. Remove the pan from the heat and stir in the other ingredients.

2 Pour the mixture into an empty, rinsed-out milk or orange juice carton and leave it to set.

3

Cut away the carton and you have a solid cake that the birds will love. Leave the bird cake whole or cut it into large chunks. You can put chunks on a bird table. Alternatively, pour the mixture into half a coconut shell to which you have added a string handle (see below), and you will be able to hang it from the washing line.

As an extra treat, thread peanuts in their shells on to lengths of string and suspend them from the bird cake or hang them from tree branches, but make sure they are out of the way of local cats!

• Ask an adult to help you to make holes in the coconut shells, thread with some string and fill with the mixture. When it has set, you can hang them up.

Indoor Projects

Time of Year – spring/summer

Growing Seeds

This is the method you need to learn to start growing many flowers, herbs, and vegetables. When the seedlings have grown, you can transfer them to the garden or use them to fill a window box, tub, or hanging basket as soon as the weather is warm enough.

You will need
• small, clean containers, such as egg boxes or yogurt pots • seed compost • seeds

3 Cover seeds with a thin layer of compost, then water gently, ideally using a watering can fitted with a rose (the piece that fits onto the end of the spout), until the compost is just moist but not too wet. Place your seed trays on a warm windowsill or near a radiator.

1 Fill containers with seed compost – but not right up to the top. Firm it down well.

2 Put seeds, well spaced, on top of the compost.

4 Water seeds when the compost begins to dry out. Never let the compost become completely dry, but do not make it soggy either. When the seedlings are about 2in (5cm) high, transfer each one to its own pot filled with potting compost.

PLANTING

Some seeds can be planted straight in the ground, where you want them to grow. The best plants for this method are hardy annuals. Choose from pot marigold (calendula), larkspur (annual delphinium), sunflowers, candytuft, love-in-a-mist (nigella), tobacco plants, and nasturtiums.

Sow these seeds any time in the spring or summer as long as it is not frosty. Before sowing, prepare the ground by raking it and removing as many stones and twigs as possible.

• Seeds need warmth, air, and moisture to germinate. They also need gentle handling once they have sprouted. When transferring seedlings to a new pot, handle them by their leaves, not by their fragile stems. Better still, scoop up the soil surrounding their roots and transfer seedling and soil to its new home.

• When buying seeds to grow by this method, look for half-hardy annuals. These include flowers such as alyssum, night-scented stocks, French marigolds, poppies, snapdragons (antirrhinum), *Impatiens*, petunias, and lobelia, all of which are extremely easy to grow.

• Seed packets have lots of information about where and when to plant. Save the packets in a scrap book.

Time of Year – spring

Beanstalk Jar

This is a great way to see how seeds germinate. Start with just a few seeds and try to guess which one will sprout first and which will grow the tallest.

You will need
- broad bean, pole bean or pea seeds
- large glass jar with lid
- kitchen paper, kitchen cloth or blotting paper

1

Half-fill the jar with tepid water and add your seeds. Leave to soak overnight.

2

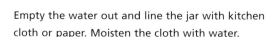

Empty the water out and line the jar with kitchen cloth or paper. Moisten the cloth with water.

3

Push the soaked seeds down between the cloth and the glass. Pour a little water into the jar, to just cover the bottom. Replace the lid. Add more water as often as necessary. In a few days you will see roots beginning to appear

4

Shoots will sprout from the seeds, followed by a pair of tiny leaves growing from each shoot. When this happens, plant each seedling in a small pot filled with potting compost.

When each little plant is about 2in (5cm) high, you can transplant them to the garden.

Time of Year – anytime

Salad Sprouts

Here is a simple way to grow a crop of crunchy salad – and you don't need a garden or even a windowsill.

You will need
- large glass jar
- mung beans
- piece of muslin or kitchen cloth
- rubber band

Put about 1 tablespoon of mung beans in the jar, cover with a little tepid water, and seal the top of the jar with the fabric, stretched tight and held in place with a rubber band.

1

SUPER SALAD SPROUTS

You can sprout a variety of beans or seeds in this way. Try alfalfa seeds, fenugreek seeds, adzuki beans, whole wheat grains, or whole lentils. Each will produce different sized sprouts and each has a distinctive flavor.

2

Leave overnight, then tip up the jar so the water drains out through the fabric. Add fresh water every morning and evening, draining the water out immediately. You will soon see the beans begin to sprout and grow.

When the sprouts are about 1–1 1/2in (3–4cm) long, you can eat them. Give them a rinse in cold water, then add to sandwich fillings and salads. Mung bean sprouts can also be used in Chinese dishes.

Time of Year – anytime

Crazy Cress

Cress seeds will sprout on damp absorbent cotton or kitchen paper and give you a little crop of salad in a matter of days.

1 Put several sheets of kitchen paper on a plate or tray. Add water to dampen – but do not make the paper too soggy. Sprinkle a layer of cress seeds on top. Write your name or a message with the seeds, or make a simple design using a paper template or a cookie cutter.

2 Your seeds should begin to sprout in a couple of days. Keep the paper moist by spraying it lightly with water. When the cress has grown to $1^1/2$–2in (4–5cm) high, it is ready to harvest – simply snip it off with scissors.

Sprinkle the cress over a salad, or put it in sandwiches on its own or with cream cheese or egg mayonnaise. Or why not combine it with some sprouted seeds (see pages 46 and 47).

EGG HEADS

Here's another fun idea. Fill a clean, empty egg shell with damp absorbent cotton. Paint a face on the shell, sprinkle seeds on the absorbent cotton, and watch your little egg head grow cress 'hair.'

You could hollow out one end of a length of summer squash, fill with damp absorbent cotton or kitchen paper, and sow cress seeds. Make a funny face on the squash by cutting slices of carrot and pepper for eyes, a peapod or slice of red pepper for a mouth, and perhaps a piece of yellow pepper for a nose, attaching them with wooden toothpicks.

Time of Year – anytime

Windowsill Herbs

Buy small plants from a garden center in spring, or grow your own herbs from seed. It's fun to plant each different herb in its own terracotta pot.

You will need
- small terracotta flowerpots
- poster paints, emulsion, or acrylic paint
- paintbrush
- drainage crocks
- potting compost
- herb plants

1 Wash the pots. For stubborn sticky labels, soak in water, then rub with washing-up liquid or washing powder, scrubbing with a nailbrush to remove all traces of glue. Paint the outside of each pot with poster paint, emulsion, or acrylic paint. When dry, you could paint the name of your chosen herb on the rim or the main part of the pot.

2 Put some crocks in the bottom of each pot.

3

Add a little compost, carefully transfer the herb plants from the pots in which you bought them and fill in any gaps with more compost, pressing it down firmly. Water the plants well.

HERBS GALORE

Here are some herbs you may like to try. Some will grow better than others, depending on the conditions. For instance, basil likes warmth and will not enjoy a cold, drafty windowsill.

Chives can be snipped with scissors to season a baked potato. Try pulling out a single stem and pushing it into a small pot of compost. If you are lucky, it will take root and produce a new plant.

Lemon verbena is deliciously lemony. Shred the leaves and sprinkle them, along with any of the tiny white flowers, over ice cream. Or add some sprigs to a glass of lemon soda. If you rub the leaves on your skin, the juice acts as an insect repellent.

Stand each pot on a saucer, or put a layer of gravel on a tray and put the pots on top.

Time of Year – spring

Beautiful Bulbs

Hyacinths, crocuses, or narcissi will all grow in water. You can either use a special glass container with a narrow neck, improvise by placing a ring of cardboard to support the bulb on top of a drinking glass, or place the bulbs on top of pebbles, shells, or marbles in a bowl of water.

Whichever method you choose, the base of the bulb should barely touch the surface of the water. If bulbs become wet, they will rot.

• Store your bulbs in a dry place. If they become damp, they will go moldy. If this happens, you may be able to save them by peeling off the outer, papery brown layer of skin.

• It is best to start bulbs off in a cool, dark place such as a cupboard. Transfer them to a cool, light spot once the green shoots appear. Then, when flowers start to grow, you can transfer them to a warm room.

• Bulbs are easily grown in soil and make great additions to window boxes.

BULBS IN THE GARDEN

Of course, you do not have to grow bulbs in water. You could put them in a pot of compost, or simply plant them in the garden. If you plant them in the ground, dig a fairly deep hole three times the size of the bulb. Place the bulb pointed side up. Cover it with soil or compost.

Carrot Tops

Time of Year – anytime

Here's a clever way to grow lots of fern-like foliage from root vegetable tops that we usually throw away.

You will need
- shallow flowerpot or similar container
- vermiculite (*see box*)
- carrots

1
Fill a shallow flowerpot with vermiculite. Cut the top off a carrot and push it down into the vermiculite until the carrot stalk is level with the surface.

2
Moisten with water and place the pot in a warm, dark place.

3 Check every day, adding a little water to keep the vermiculite damp. When green shoots appear in a few days, move the pot into a light position. Spray with water regularly.

For an attractive display, why not grow carrot tops all round the edge of a large flowerpot, then place a flowering plant, such as a geranium, in a smaller pot of compost in the center?

GREAT GRAVEL

Vermiculite is a special kind of fine lightweight gravel, available from garden centers. If you do not have any, try starting off your carrot top on damp kitchen paper.

The larger the carrot, the more foliage it will produce. Turnips, parsnips, and radishes work too. Try growing a selection, then compare the difference in the color and shape of the leaves.

Bottle Garden

Time of Year – anytime

Almost any large glass container can be turned into a table-top conservatory. You may find a suitable jar in a rummage or garage sale, or even have something at home – an unused goldfish bowl, storage jar or drink flask, for example.

• Plants to choose from include ferns and mosses, small-leaved ivies, scarlet pimpernel, African violet, sedum, miniature roses, and many other small house plants.
• Choose a variety of leaf shapes and colors for a really interesting display.
• Protected from dust and drafts, plants enjoy the atmosphere inside a glass container and, as condensation forms on the 'roof' of the container and drips back down, this means you do not have to water your garden very frequently.

You will need
• large glass container
• small pebbles or gravel
• stiff paper
• potting compost
• long-handled trowel, fork or spoon and stick
• various small plants

1 Start with a layer of small pebbles, to help drainage. Drop them into the container gently so you do not crack the glass. It helps if you tilt the container and roll them in.

2 To stop the compost sticking to the inside of the glass, roll the paper into a cone, put it in the neck of the jar, and pour in potting compost. The compost should be about 2-3in (5-8cm) deep.

3 Slide the plants, one by one, through the paper cone and into planting holes that you have made.

4 Tie a fork or spoon to a long stick. You can use it to make holes and to position the plants.

5 After planting, spray in just a little water.

Time of Year – anytime

Wiggly Wormery

Worms are essential to the balance of nature in a garden. They burrow under the earth, carrying dead leaves and other plant material with them, which nourishes the soil. And the tunnels they create help to break up the ground and allow water and air to penetrate and reach the roots of plants.

To see how worms do their valuable work, try making a worm observatory.

You will need
- transparent container
- fine sand
- garden soil
- earthworms
- leaves and grass
- brown paper or newspaper

1

Fill a large glass or acrylic jar, goldfish bowl, or tank with alternate ³/4in (2cm) layers of sand and soil.

2

Dig up some earthworms from the ground and place them on top with some leaves and grass.

When you remove the paper, you should see patterns where the sand and soil layers have been disturbed as the worms have moved around.

4

3

Wrap the sides of the tank with paper, to keep out the light. Wait patiently for a few days. Ensure the soil is kept moist but not too wet.

5

Do remember to handle the worms gently and return them to the soil when you have finished observing them.

Time of Year – anytime

Colorful Carnations

Try this experiment and see for yourself how plants 'drink' water, sucking it up via thin tubes within their stems. It is called transpiration.

You will need:
- glass bottle or jar
- food coloring
- white carnations

1 Fill a bottle or jar with water and add a few drops of food coloring – any color you like.

Put the stems of white carnations into the bottle. The flower will start to draw up water through its stem almost immediately. See what happens to the petals!

2

If you have a bunch of white carnations, why not dye each one a different color?

• You could try this: split the stem of a single flower from the bottom almost up to the flower head and put each half in a jar of differently colored water.

Record the results of your experiment in your gardening notebook. How long does it take before the flower petals change color?

RED CELERY

Place a celery stalk in a jar of water to which you have added a little red food coloring.

Leave it overnight and you will find that the leaves have turned red in places. Cut the stalk in half and you will see red spots where the colored water has traveled up it.

Flower Arranging

Pick a few flowers from the garden so you can enjoy them inside the house as well. You could arrange them in a vase or create a posy as a gift.

Time of Year – anytime

You will need
- a selection of colorful flowers with stems about 8in (20cm) long
- raffia
- tissue paper or paper doily
- ribbon

1 Start with two flowers, crossing the stems in the middle. Then add another and another, turning the bunch as you go. When you have about ten flowers, tie the stems at the point where they cross, using a small length of raffia.

2 Carry on adding more flowers until you are pleased with your posy, then get another piece of raffia and tie the stems again.

ARTISTIC ARRANGEMENTS

So that flowers remain where you position them, it helps to have something in the container to hold the stems in place. Florists use a special foam block but if you do not have any, try putting some pebbles or marbles in the container or ask a grown-up to crumple up a piece of chicken wire and push this into the vase.

If you like, you can wrap the stems in tissue paper, or cut a hole in the center of a lacy paper doily and push the stems through. To finish off, tie a bow with some ribbon around the posy.

Time of Year – anytime

Grassy Granny

It is easy to make this funny head with its green hair. Stand it in a plastic pot or the bottom cut off a plastic bottle and decorate it in any way you like.

You will need
- old panty hose
- grass seed
- string or rubber bands
- sawdust • plastic pot

1 Cut a 10in (25cm) length from the leg of a pair of panty hose. Tie one end or fasten it with a rubber band, and turn it inside out.

2 Pour in 2 tablespoons of grass seed, then add about 3 or 4 cups of sawdust. Tie another knot. On one side, push out a nose shape and tie with string or secure with a rubber band.

3 Cut features from paper, felt, or colored plastic sheet, or stick on plastic goggly eyes (available from craft shops). Stand the head in a plastic pot. Sprinkle with water every day and watch the grass hair grow!